AF585262

Australia's Neighbours

Myanmar

(Burma)

DISCOVER THE COUNTRY, CULTURE AND PEOPLE

Jane Hinchey

First published 2019 by
Redback Publishing
PO Box 357 Frenchs Forest NSW 2086
Australia

www.redbackpublishing.com.au
orders@redbackpublishing.com.au

978-1-925630-84-8

Author: Jane Hinchey
Editor: Marianne Lindsell
Designer: Redback Publishing

MIX
Paper from responsible sources
FSC www.fsc.org
FSC® C020056

Original illustrations © Redback Publishing 2019
Originated by Redback Publishing

Printed and bound in China by Leo Paper

Acknowledgements
Abbreviations: l—left, r—right, b—bottom, t—top, c—centre, m—middle
We would like to thank the following for permission to reproduce photographs: (Images © shutterstock) p10bl Apik, p11b Hafiz Johari, p12b Pavel Svoboda, p16 Phuong D. Nguyen, p17 Stephane Bidouze, p21 360b, p29b Sudpoth Sirirattanasakul

Every effort has been made to contact copyright holders of any material reproduced in this book. Any omissions will be rectified in subsequent printings if notice is given to the publisher.

A catalogue record for this book is available from the National Library of Australia

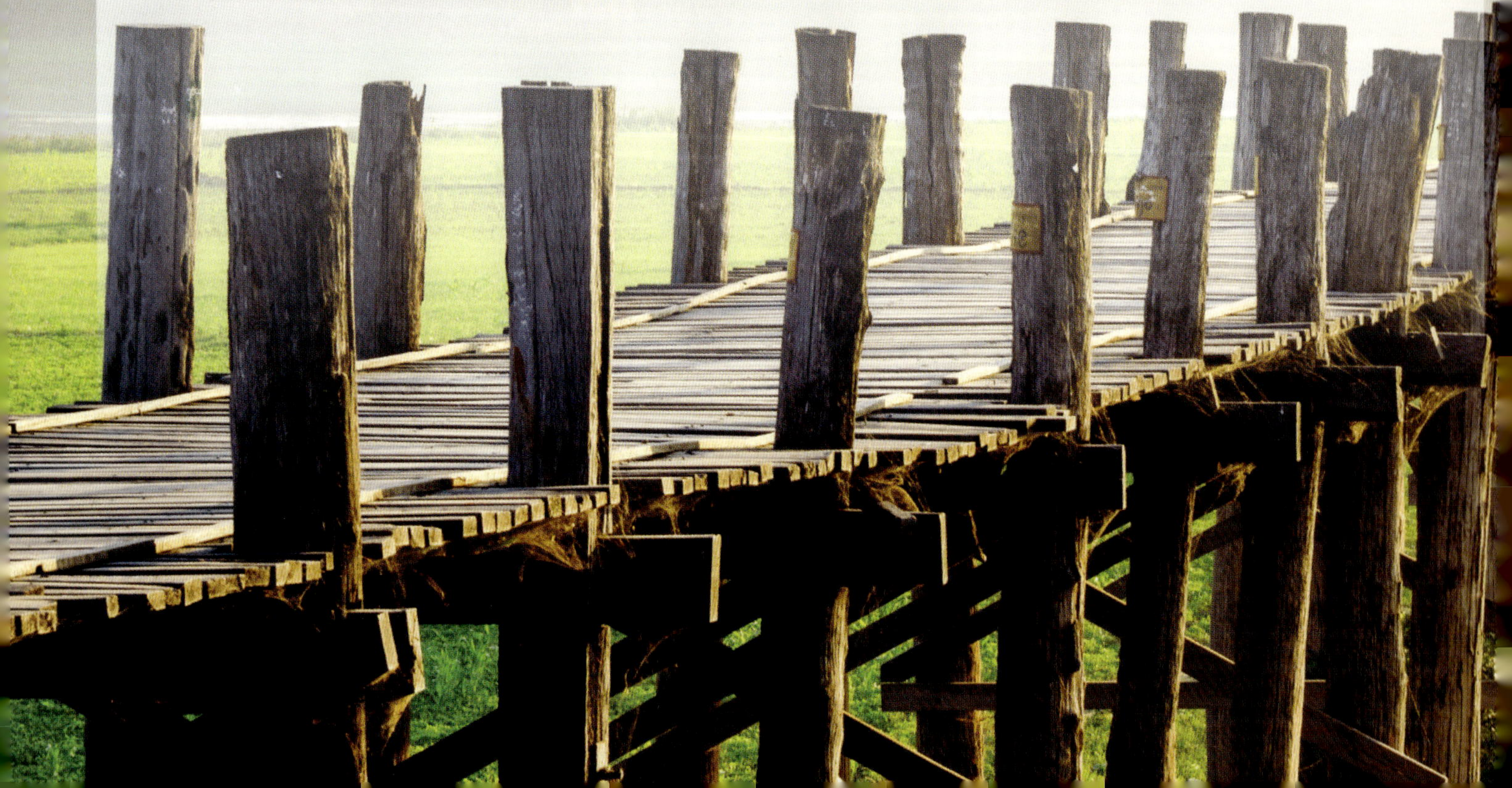

Contents

Map of Myanmar

Snapshot

Country name:	Republic of the Union of Myanmar (formerly known as Burma)
Independence:	4 January 1948
Population:	53,993,000 (2018)
Government:	Unitary parliamentary constitutional republic
Capital:	Nay Pyi Taw (Naypyidaw)
Area:	676,578 square kilometres
Official Language:	Burmese
Main Religion:	Buddhism
Currency:	Burmese kyat

MAJOR SITES

- Yangon
- Bagan
- Mandalay
- Inle Lake
- Shwedagon Pagoda
- Kyaiktiyo Pagoda
- Ananda Temple
- Mount Popa
- Kandawgyi Lake
- Golden Rock Pagoda

Fun Facts

- Myanmar has two names. Officially it is called Myanmar, but when people talk about the country in an unofficial way, they call it Burma.
- Myanmar is one of only three countries not to adopt the metric system of measurement. Liberia and the USA are the other two.
- The Intha people on Inle Lake grow vegetables on floating islands made of weeds and water hyacinth.

Meet the Neighbour: Myanmar

The Republic of the Union of Myanmar, also known as Burma, is in Southeast Asia. It is bordered by India and Bangladesh to its west, Thailand and Laos to its east, and China to its north and northeast.

Australia and Myanmar have an important partnership. Myanmar's capital city, Nay Pyi Taw (Naypyidaw) is 8,284 kilometres away from Australia's capital city, Canberra. Australia has had diplomatic relations with Myanmar since 1952.

The first Myanmar people to settle in Australia were called 'Anglo-Burmese', and of Myanmar and European descent. Myanmar was administered by the British from 1886 as Burma, but following independence from Britain in 1948 many Anglo-Burmese left.

Between 1947 and 1959, about 3,500 Anglo-Burmese settled in Australia. Another 2,500 arrived in 1962 after the military takeover of the Myanmar government. A further 2,500 Anglo-Burmese settled in Australia between 1965 and 1972. By 1991, the Census recorded 8,223 Myanmar-born people in Australia. Today there are around 30,000 Myanmar-born people in Australia.

A Complex Issue

Despite Australian allies such as the USA, UK, Canada, France and the EU cutting ties with Myanmar's military over its violence against Rohingya Muslims, in 2017 and 2018 Australia's Department of Defence spent around $400,000 on English lessons and training courses for members of the Myanmar military.

Australian Aid

Australian aid helps promote stability in Myanmar. In 2018-19 Australian Official Development Assistance (ODA) will be approximately $76.9 million.

Australia's ODA supports local initiatives with a particular focus on education and building economic resilience among the poorest and most marginalised communities.

The main objectives of Australian aid are:

- to enhance human development by improving education access and learning outcomes
- to promote peace and stability
- to promote inclusive economic growth and government management.

In 2017-18 Australian Aid was linked to:

- over 10 million Myanmar students benefiting from grants to 47,000 government and monastic schools
- stipends to 46,605 disadvantaged students, 53.6% of them female, which enabled them to continue their education
- increased finance that helped 124,000 people; 90% of them rural women
- humanitarian assistance to 397,772 people (at least 44% estimated to be women) in Rakhine, Kachin, northern Shan and on the Thai border.

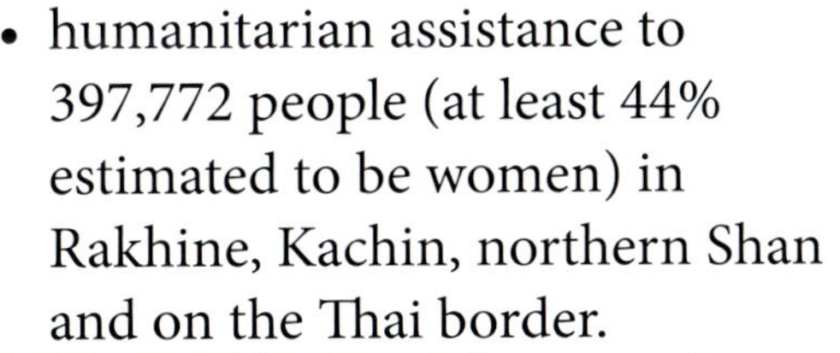

Australia Awards

Australia Awards are prestigious scholarships and fellowships funded by the Australian government. In 2019, 3,186 individuals from 55 developing countries have been offered placements. Currently, there are 98 scholars from Myanmar studying in Australia on an Australia Award.

At a Glance

Myanmar is a Unitary Parliamentary Constitutional Republic. The country was ruled by a military junta led by General Ne Win from 1962 to 1988. In 2016 Htin Kyaw became the first elected civilian leader, although the role of President is largely ceremonial. In 2018, Win Myint became President.

Aung San Suu Kyi, the long-term leader of the pro-democracy movement, was prevented from becoming President by the constitution of Myanmar because her children were British citizens. Instead, she acts as an advisor to the President.

Despite these more recent political changes in Myanmar, the military remains in control.

In 2017, the World Bank classified Myanmar as a lower middle economy, although between 2005 and 2015 there has been a reduction in poverty, from 48% to 32%. The Rakhine conflict has also wwcaused some inflation and currency depreciation, however in 2017 and 2018 the economy still grew by 6.4%.

Agricultural processing, cement, fertiliser, pharmaceuticals, wood and wood products, copper, tin, tungsten, iron, construction materials, petroleum and natural gas, garments, jade and gems.

Rice, beans, pulses and maize.

Tin, copper, zinc, tungsten, and precious stones such as jade, rubies and sapphires.

Main Imports

Myanmar's main import partners are China, Thailand, Singapore and Japan.
Its main imports are:

- fabric
- petroleum products
- plastics
- fertiliser
- machinery
- transport equipment
- cement
- construction materials
- crude oil
- food products
- edible oil

Main Exports

Myanmar shipped $16.4 billion worth of goods around the globe in 2017. Its top export partners are China, Thailand, India and Japan.
Its top exports are:

- mineral fuels including oil
- clothing and accessories
- vegetables
- sugar and sugar confectionery
- cereals
- fish
- gems and precious metals
- machinery including computers
- oil seeds
- copper

Among the top 10 export categories, machinery including computers was the fastest-growing segment, up by a whopping 1,858% from 2016 to 2017.

People

Myanmar has a population of over 54 million people. Most of the population and agricultural lands are found along the Irrawaddy River basin (officially the Ayeyarwady River). The citizens of Myanmar are called Myanmars or Myanmarese, however there are many ethnic groups within this. The majority are Bamar and live primarily in the central lowlands, while the other ethnic groups live mainly in the highlands.

The government identifies eight major ethnic races living in Myanmar. Within these eight groups, 135 ethnic subgroups are officially recognised, making Myanmar one of Asia's most ethnically diverse countries.

Bamar

Around two-thirds of the population are Bamar, who primarily live in the Irrawaddy. They migrated to the area from Yunnan, China in the 7th century. The Bamar speak Burmese, which is also the national language of Myanmar. The Bamar dominate Myanmar's government and the military.

Sea Gypsies

The Moken are a sub-group within the Bamar ethnic race. They are nomadic and live in huts on the water around the Mergui (or Myeik) Archipelago in Myanmar's far south. Famous for their free diving skills, the Moken are also called Salon, or sea gypsies.

Myanmar's Recognised Ethnic Groups:

- 68% Bamar
- 9% Shan
- 7% Karen
- 4% Rakhine
- 3% Chinese
- 2% Indian
- 2% Mon
- 5% other

Rakhine

Rakhine people account for 4% of the population of Myanmar. They were subjected to a forced assimilation policy and forbidden from speaking their language from 1962 until 2015. Rakhine people are very talented weavers and the majority practice Buddhism.

Most Rakhine live in the western coastal state of Rakhine. They made international headlines in 2017 when Rakhine-Rohingya conflicts saw a military crackdown force more than 600,000 Rohingya into neighbouring Bangladesh.

Unrecognised People

There are a number of minority groups that are not recognised by the Myanmar government. These include the Burmese Chinese, Lisu, Rawang, Naga, Padaung Panthay, Burmese Indians, Rohingya, Anglo-Burmese and Gurkha. In total, Myanmar's unrecognised groups form around 10% of the country's population.

Rohingya

One unrecognised minority is the Rohingya. The Rohingya speak Rohingya or Ruaingga. They are predominantly Muslim, although a small percentage are Hindu.

Before 2016, there were an estimated one million Rohingya living in Myanmar. However, a military crackdown meant that by December 2017, an estimated 700,000 Rohingya refugees from Rakhine had crossed the border into Bangladesh. The United Nations says the Rohingya are one of the most persecuted minorities in the world.

Daily Life

Family is important in Myanmar and people often live in multi-generational homes, especially in rural areas. Young people are expected to respect their elders and take care of them when they are old. While women are considered equal in Burmese society, men are still considered to be head of the family while women take responsibility for raising children and running the home.

Health

According to the World Health Organization (WHO), Myanmar's healthcare expenditure is one of the lowest in the world. There is an increase in tobacco and alcohol-related illnesses, illicit drug use and related medical conditions. However, the government has recently prioritised healthcare and has announced plans to achieve universal health coverage by 2030. Some organisations are addressing the broader issues involved in maintaining good health, such as sanitation, clean water and nutrition.

Myanmar has fewer doctors per capita than most countries in the region. Apart from in Yangon and Mandalay, hospitals are underfunded and ill equipped. In rural areas, health centres are often limited to providing basic services and are run by poorly trained supervisors.

Education

The education system is based on the United Kingdom's system, due to nearly a century of British colonial rule. Primary school is compulsory and lasts five years. To attend high school, students must pass examinations. School uniforms are mandatory and places in better schools are often reserved for children of those with government connections.

Traditional Houses

Traditional rural homes are made of wood or palm thatch. The house is lifted above the ground on stilts. This lifts the home above any flooding, and also lets air circulate when it's humid. The front of the house usually has a veranda where guests are entertained. In many of the older houses there is no indoor plumbing. Buddhist altars are found in the main room of the home, and shoes are removed at the front door.

Clothes

Many people now wear western style clothes; however the national dress is still popular. Myanmar's men and women wear either a pasoe or htamein both of which are considered to be a longyi. The longyi is a piece of cloth sewn into a cylindrical tube, slipped over the head by men and stepped into by the women. Men knot the longyi in front and women tie it to the side. The longyi comes in a variety of materials and colours, including velvet, silk, lace, muslin, and cotton. Mon and Rakhine people also wear the longyi, while other ethnic groups have their own costumes.

Burmese Names

There are no family surnames in Burmese. Children are given names using astrological calculations, or a method where days of the week are assigned to various letters of the alphabet. Women also keep their maiden names when they marry, however names can change according to circumstances.

က ခ ဂ ဃ င
စ ဆ ဇ ဈ ည
ဋ ဌ ဍ ဎ ဏ
တ ထ ဒ ဓ န
ပ ဖ ဗ ဘ မ
ယ ရ လ ဝ သ
ဟ ဠ အ

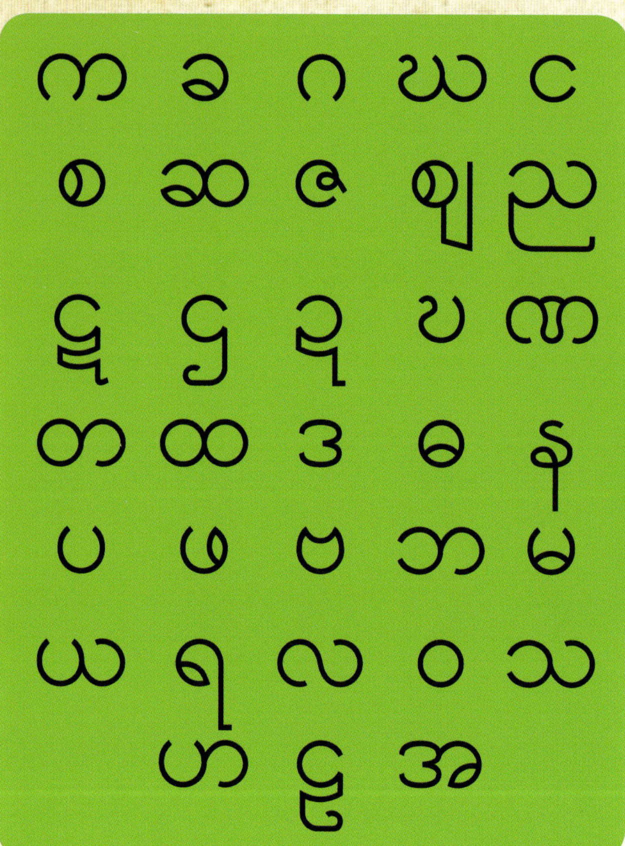

Language

Burmese is the official language of Myanmar. It is a tonal language, like Chinese and Thai. The way it is pronounced affects its meaning. The tones are indicated in writing using diacritics or special letters.

Myanmar Script

The Burmese or Myanmar script developed from the Mon script, which was adapted from Brahmi script from India.

There are also around 111 other indigenous languages in Myanmar. Some languages are spoken by only a few hundred people while languages such as Karen and Shan are spoken by millions. English was the official language during the colonial period. Burmese, Chinese and Hindi were the languages of commerce. At the end of the colonial period, in 1962, Burmese became the official language and English ceased to be important. In recent years, people are being encouraged to study it again.

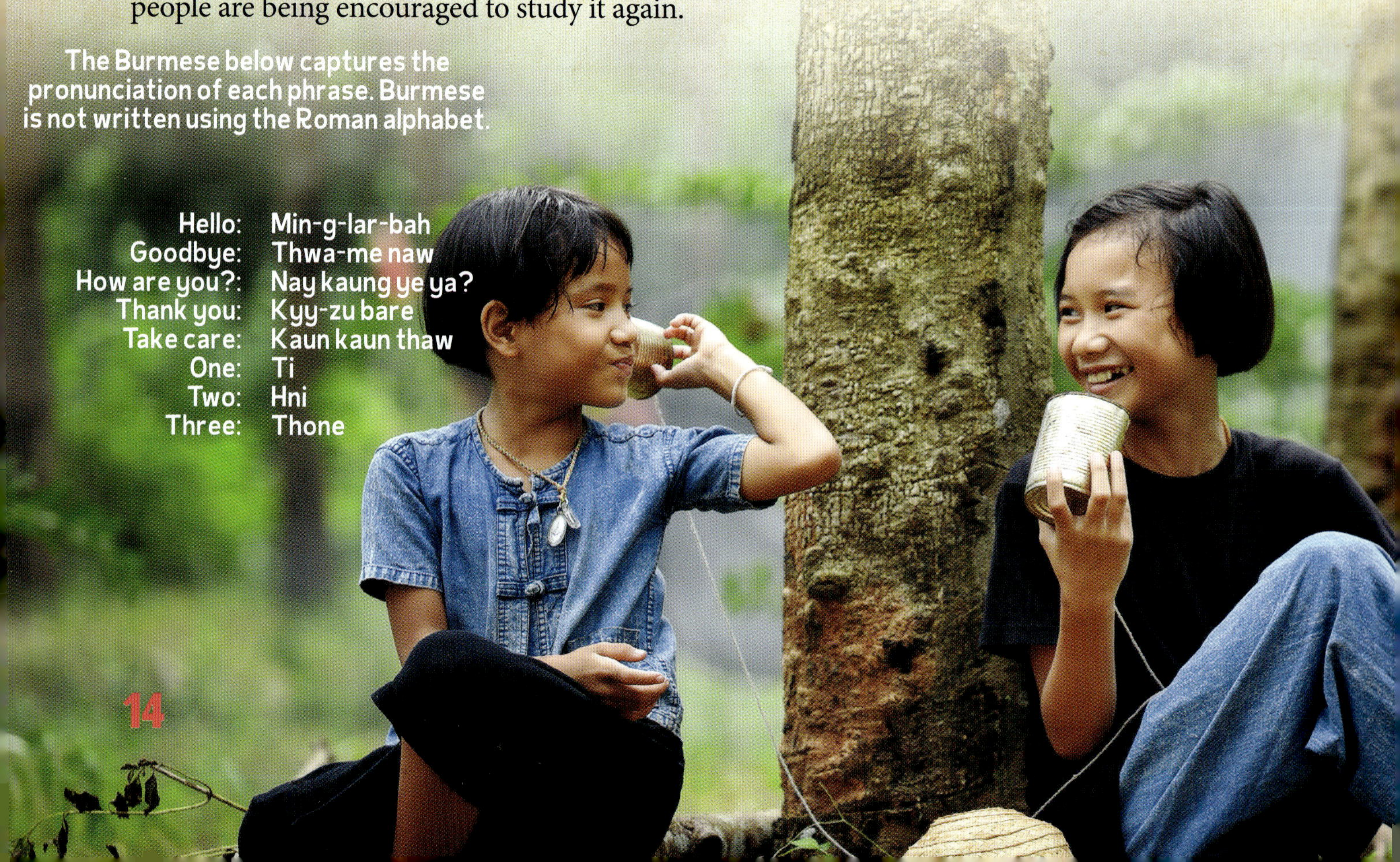

The Burmese below captures the pronunciation of each phrase. Burmese is not written using the Roman alphabet.

Hello:	Min-g-lar-bah
Goodbye:	Thwa-me naw
How are you?:	Nay kaung ye ya?
Thank you:	Kyy-zu bare
Take care:	Kaun kaun thaw
One:	Ti
Two:	Hni
Three:	Thone

Traditional Arts

Myanmar has a rich history of traditional arts influenced heavily by exposure to nearby cultures. Regional and rural art forms include lacquerware, metalwork, woodcarving, silverwork and goldwork, weaving and basket making, and wood and ivory carving. Buddhism and Hinduism also play a large role in cultural and intellectual life.

There are 10 main traditional arts which are called the Ten Flowers:

- Panbe (the art of blacksmith)
- Panbu (the art of sculpture)
- Pantain (the art of gold and silver smith)
- Pantin (the art of bronze casting)
- Pantaut (the art of making floral designs using masonry)
- Panyan (the art of bricklaying and masonry)
- Pantamault (the art of sculpting with stone)
- Panpoot (the art of turning designs on the lathe)
- Panchi (the art of painting)
- Panyun (the art of making lacquerware)

Puppetry

Traditional Burmese puppet theatre, called yoke thay, dates from the 15th century. Puppets were a way to pass on tradition as they recounted tales and fables, and also to share social and political messages. During the show, the master puppeteer manipulates up to 28 dolls, some with 60 strings. While not as popular as it was in the past, there is a push to make this popular again, before this important tradition is lost forever.

A City Life Survey by the Asia Foundation in 2017 found that women have the same education opportunities as men, but bear more domestic responsibilities.

Life in Cities

About 30% of Myanmar's population live in cities. Many people have migrated to urban areas looking for work.

Myanmar's two largest cities are Yangon and Mandalay, with populations of 5 million and 1.5 million respectively. Recent economic growth means there is a focus on building new infrastructure, and tourism and foreign investment has brought with it a buzzing café and restaurant scene to both cities.

Finishing off the top 5 largest cities are Naypyidaw with a population of 924,608, and Taunggyi and Mawlamyine, with populations under 500,000.

Generally, life in urban areas is like any other country with good amenities, entertainment options and shopping.

Life in Rural Areas

About 70% of Myanmar's population lives in rural areas. Life there can be tough, with many people living below the poverty line. Infrastructure is almost non-existent in many areas, while others have only basic public services. Less than 40% of people in rural areas have electricity. Many don't have access to safe drinking water and sanitation facilities. Young people move to cities looking for work, often in neighbouring countries like Thailand, Malaysia and Singapore.

For those in rural communities, their way of life has not changed much for generations. People live simple lives, maintaining a faith in Buddhist teachings. Community spirit is strong, with many annual festivals and family and community events. Families still live in traditional style homes and own farms or small businesses. Many generations live under one roof.

Villages are usually small, and the residents are farmers, or fishermen in coastal areas. Crops are farmed on land that spreads out from the village to the areas surrounding around it. There are no fences and farmers work with oxen, connected to ploughs with a yoke. The Buddhist temple is at the centre of life for the residents.

Natural Disasters

Myanmar is one of the world's most disaster-prone countries. The most common natural disasters to affect the country are floods, cyclones, earthquakes, landslides and droughts.

Myanmar's History

Timeline

1057

King Anawrahta defeats the Mon Kingdom and creates the first Burmese empire. He adopts Theravada Buddhism.

1287

The Mongols, under Kublai Khan, conquer the first Burmese empire.

1755

Alaungpaya founds the Konbaung dynasty.

The Anglo-Burmese Wars

Between 1824 and 1826, British India joins with Siam (now Thailand) and attacks Burma. The first Anglo-Burmese war ends with the Treaty of Yandabo, and the British controlling parts of Burma's coastal strip, between Chittagong and Cape Negrais. In 1852, after the second Anglo-Burmese war, Britain annexes lower Burma, including Rangoon. In 1885, after the third Anglo-Burmese war, Britain controls the whole country, and Burma becomes a province of British India. In 1937, Britain separates Burma from India and makes it a crown colony.

The Second World War

In 1942, Japan invades Burma with help from the Japanese-trained Burma Independence Army, led by Aung San. In 1943, Aung Sun changes the Burma Independence Army into the Anti-Fascist People's Freedom League (AFPFL) and negotiates Burma's independence from Britain. In 1945, Britain and the AFPFL liberate Burma from Japanese occupation.

Australia and Burma in The Second World War

During the Second World War, the Japanese invaded Burma. Japan wanted to cut overland access to China from Burma via the famed Burma Road. Japan also planned to invade India. Getting supplies by sea to their forces in Burma was risky, so it was decided they would build a railway.

The Thai-Burma Railway

Following the fall of Singapore in 1942, the Japanese took 22,000 Australians prisoner. Many of these were sent to Thailand to work on the railway, also known as the Death Railway because of the appalling conditions.

More than 60,000 Allied prisoners and about 200,000 Asian labourers were used to build it. The railway was to run 420 kilometres through rugged jungle, and included an area of pure rock known as the Hellfire Pass in Thailand. The Japanese wanted the railway finished as quickly as possible, so the POWs (Prisoners of War) and labourers were forced to work shifts of up to 33-hours, with very little food and only hand tools. The men had to clear dense rainforest and build embankments for tracks to be laid. In June 1943, monsoonal rains created an environment where disease spread, clothes and shoes fell apart, and the food they ate was already rotten. About a quarter of the workers died because of overwork, malnutrition, and diseases like cholera, malaria and dysentery. Others were beaten to death by guards.

About 90,000 labourers and 12,000 POWs, including 2,700 Australians, died due to harsh conditions and appalling treatment. The surviving POWs were moved to Singapore when the railway was completed.

Australian RAAF

Over 1,000 members of the Royal Australian Air Force served on the India-Burma front, spread among more than 60 of Britain's Royal Air Force (RAF) squadrons. Many fought the Japanese and five RAAF pilots were regarded as fighter 'aces' and received the Distinguished Flying Cross while serving on the India-Burma front. Australia's RAAF presence played a significant part in bringing about the Japanese defeat in Burma.

Timeline continued...

1947
Aung San is assassinated before he can become the country's first Prime Minister.

1948
Burma becomes independent with U Nu as Prime Minister.

1962
U Nu's faction ousted in military coup and General Ne Win comes to power.

1988
Thousands of people are killed in anti-government riots.

1989
Burma is renamed the Union of Myanmar. The leader of the National League for Democracy (NLD) Aung San Suu Kyi, the daughter of Aung San, is put under house arrest.

1991
Aung San Suu Kyi is awarded the Nobel Peace Prize.

1995
Aung San Suu Kyi is released from house arrest. She is placed there again from 2000 until 2002, and then put in prison in 2003, before again being transferred to house arrest.

2016
Htin Kyaw becomes the first elected civilian leader, although the role of President is largely ceremonial. Aung San Suu Kyi, the long-term leader of the pro-democracy movement, is prevented from becoming President by the constitution of Myanmar because her children are British citizens. Instead, she acts as an advisor to the President.

2017
A military crackdown forces more than 600,000 Rohingya into neighbouring Bangladesh. The international community condemns Myanmar and Aung San Suu Kyi.

2018
Win Myint becomes President.

Aung San Suu Kyi

In March 1988, Suu Kyi the daughter of the assassinated independence leader Aung San, returned to Burma to nurse her dying mother. Suu Kyi was married to an Englishman and lived in Oxford with him and their two sons. What was expected to be a short trip back home to Burma became something else entirely. While there, she was swept up in pro-democracy protests, and found herself as leader of the opposition to the generals who had ruled Burma with great brutality for so long. Her own father was seen as the 'father of the nation', so the Burmese people embraced Suu Kyi as his successor, and the military placed her under house arrest.

In 1990, her National League for Democracy won a landslide in elections but the Burmese regime refused to accept the results. Suu Kyi spent much of her time between 1989 and 2010 in some form of detention. She stood by her people by not returning to her family in England. Her two sons grew up without her and her husband Michael died in 1999 without her there.

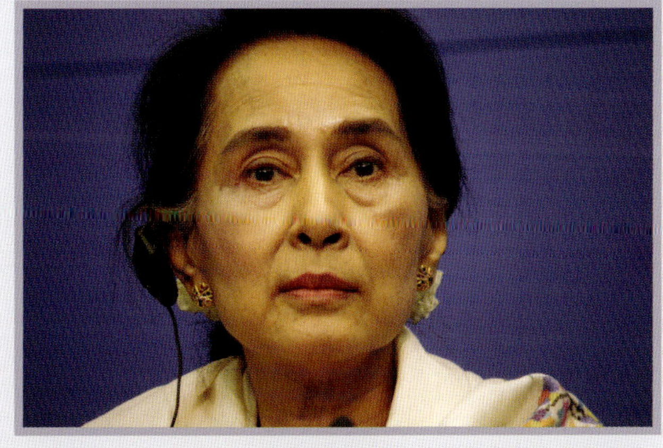

She led the National League for Democracy (NLD) to a majority win in Myanmar's first openly-contested election in 25 years in November 2015. In 2016, Htin Kyaw became the first elected civilian leader, although the role of President is largely ceremonial. Aung San Suu Kyi is prevented from becoming President by the constitution of Myanmar because her children are British citizens; so instead, she acts as an advisor to the President. Many people still see her as the leader.

Over the years, Aung San Suu Kyi was internationally celebrated, and in 1991 she was awarded the Nobel Peace Prize. However, in 2016-17 the international community turned on her when a military crackdown forced more than 600,000 Rohingya into neighbouring Bangladesh. Doctors Without Borders has estimated that the number of Rohingya killed in Myanmar's military operations is around 10,000.

Aung San Suu Kyi refused to condemn the powerful military or acknowledge accounts of atrocities.

Religion and Beliefs

In theory, Myanmar has freedom of religion, but the reality is different for some religious minorities. The majority of people are Buddhists, although Islam and Christianity have grown significantly in recent years.

Around 90% of Myanmar's population is Buddhist with the vast majority practicing Theravada Buddhism. Many young Burmese become monks or nuns for a period of time. Buddhists live by the Five Moral Precepts, which insist refraining from:

- harming living things
- taking what is not given
- sexual misconduct
- lying or gossip
- taking intoxicating substances such as drugs or drink.

While Buddhism is historically a peaceful religion, there is a militant brand of Buddhism that is growing in Myanmar.

Happy New Year

Myanmar's Buddhist calendar is filled with annual festivals. One of the most important is Thingyan, the Burmese New Year. Celebrated annually in April, Thingyan lasts for four or five days and during that time people wash away the old year by spraying water hoses, fire hydrants and even water pistols. Each evening at 6.30pm the water games stop and people enjoy sharing banquets and parties.

Swe taw myat buddha tooth relic pagoda, Yangon

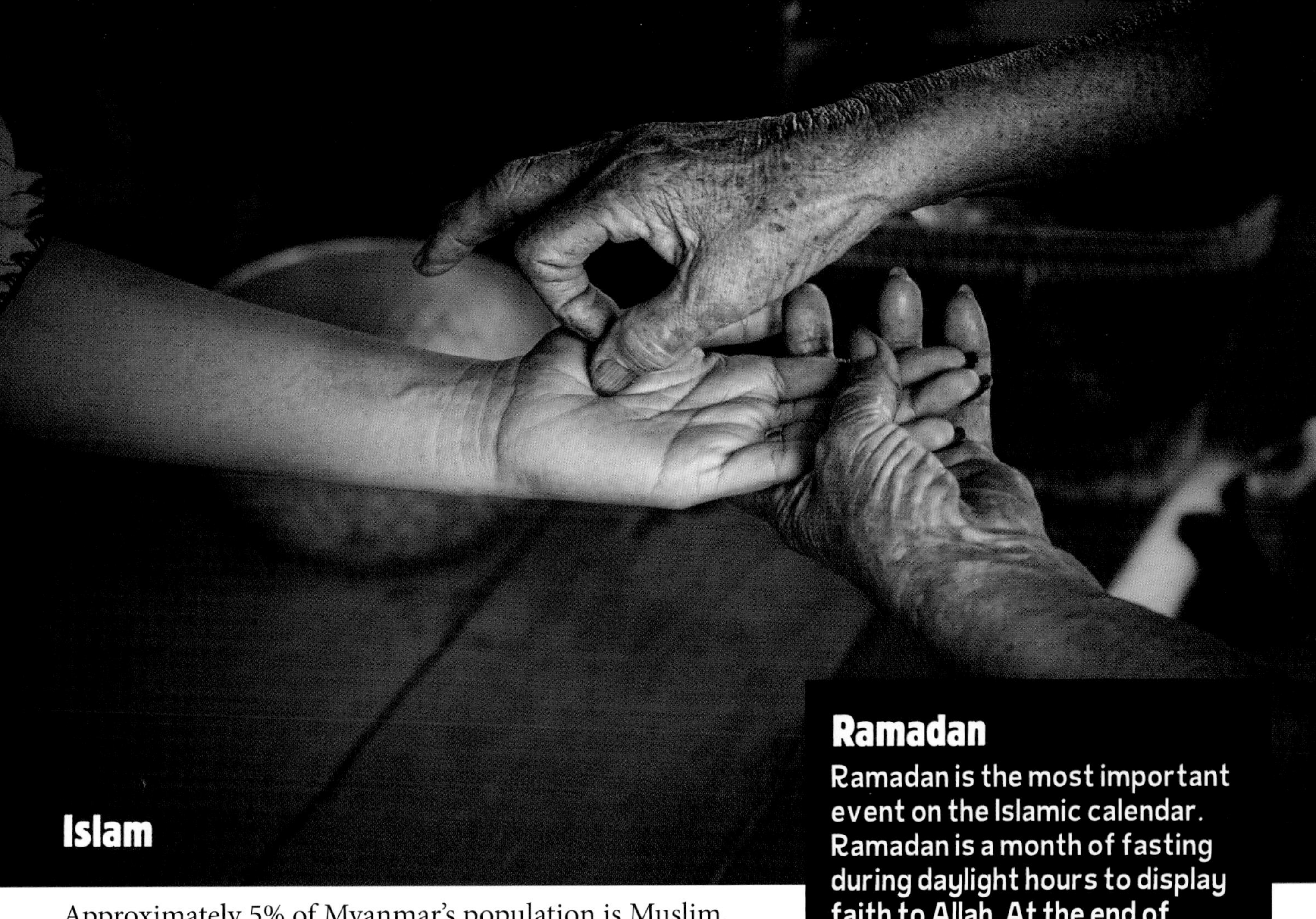

Islam

Approximately 5% of Myanmar's population is Muslim. Islam arrived in the country in the 9th century with Muslim sailors and traders. Muslims believe in one god, called Allah, who gave his message to a prophet called Mohammed. The holy book is called the Koran.

Ramadan

Ramadan is the most important event on the Islamic calendar. Ramadan is a month of fasting during daylight hours to display faith to Allah. At the end of Ramadan, there is a big three-day celebration where families and friends celebrate together.

There are a variety of Muslim ethnic minorities, including the Chinese-Muslim Panthay in northern Myanmar, Shan Muslims, and Rohingya Muslims in Rakhine. Militant Buddhists often target Muslims. In 2016-17 more than 600,000 Rohingya fled to neighbouring Bangladesh.

Christianity

About 6% of Myanmar's population is Christian. Portuguese missionaries introduced Christianity in the 1600s. Most Christians are from the minority ethnic groups such as the Chin, Karen, Lisu, Kachin, and Lahu. There are protestant and catholic Christians in Myanmar as well as a growing evangelical movement.

Fortune-telling

Many Myanmarese consult astrologers, fortune-tellers and palmists. Astrologers are consulted before making decisions about marriage or business, and also to help choose auspicious days for major events, and names for babies.

Cuisine

The cuisine of Myanmar has been heavily influenced by its neighbours. From India there is the use of chickpeas and spices such as turmeric, cumin and coriander. Chinese influences are seen in the use of soybean products and the Chinese wok, which is used for frying. While it is less spicy than Thai food, traditional Thai ingredients such as chilli, garlic, ginger, fish paste, palm sugar, lemongrass and lime juice, coconut and soy sauce are used.

Dishes vary around the country and there are regional influences. Staples are rice, noodles, tofu, fish, pork and chicken. In the central plain, people rely on freshwater fish, while in some mountainous areas, insects such as grasshoppers and ants are eaten. Clear soup (hingo) helps wash down most meals.

On The Menu

Mohinga

Regarded as Myanmar's national dish, Mohinga is a fish-based soup prepared with rice noodles. The dish has many regional variations; however, the basis for the recipe remains the same.

Lephet

A popular fermented tea leaf salad, sometimes mixed with tomatoes and nuts, or served as an appetiser.

Shan Noodles

This is one of the most famous dishes in Myanmar. Served with a sweet broth, the soup includes thin rice noodle with marinated pork or chicken.

Fabulous Fruit

Myanmar's climate is well suited to growing tropical fruit, and you'll find a wide variety of familiar and not so familiar fruits all over the country.

Durian

The strong-smelling durian is a very popular fruit, with a number of varieties.

Custard Apple

The custard apple is a cool season fruit, beloved by the Myanmarese. Inside is opaque white flesh marked with dozens of large brown seeds. The fruit is sweet and creamy in texture.

Pomelo

It looks like a giant grapefruit, but can grow up to two kilos in size. The pomelo comes in both sweet and sour varieties. They are often used in salads.

Rambutan

The rambutan is native to Southeast Asia. They are closely related to the lychee fruit. The rambutan has a hairy appearance and can be eaten straight from the tree.

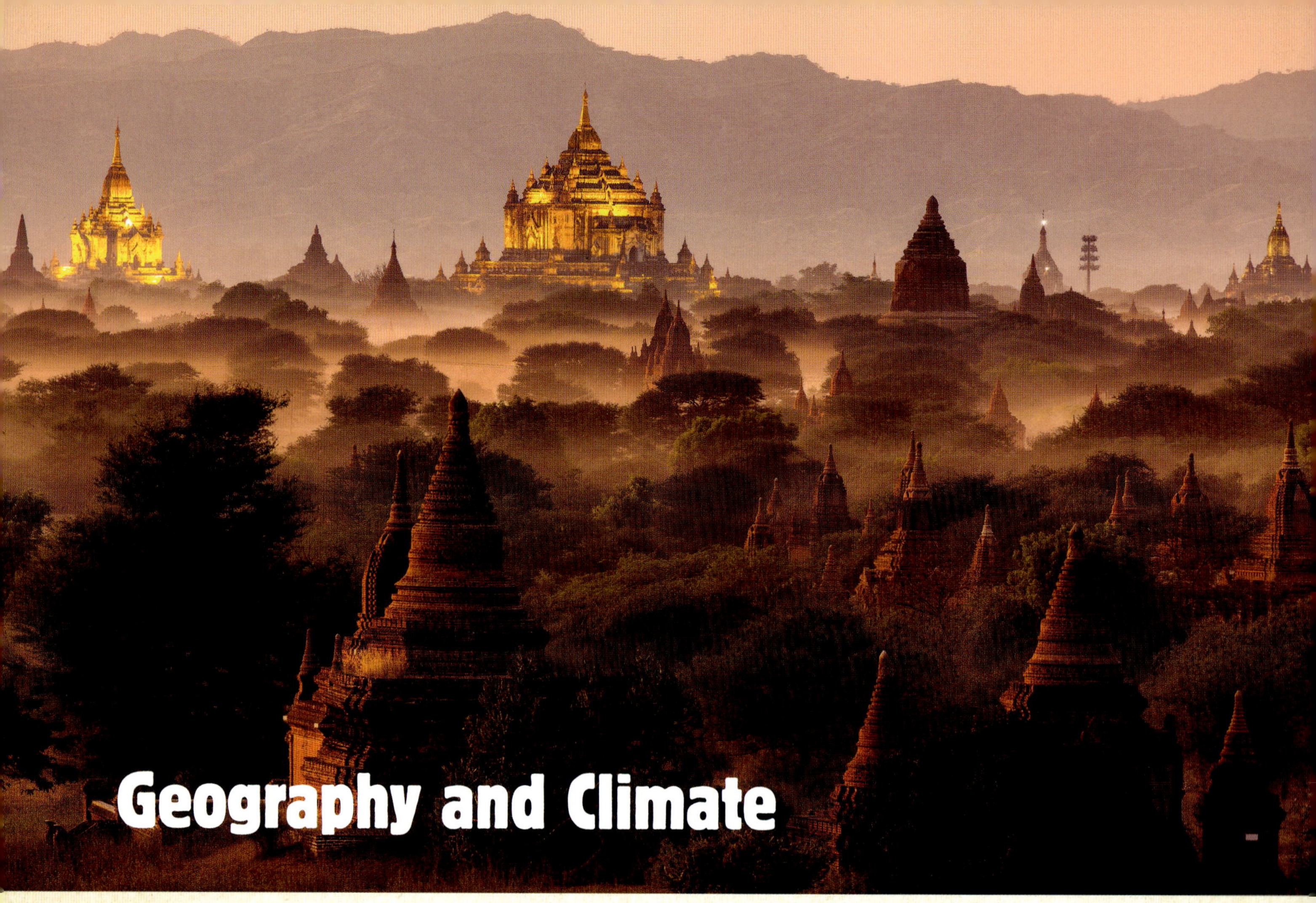

Geography and Climate

Myanmar is located in Southeast Asia, and is the region's second largest country. It shares 6,522 kilometres of its borders with India, Bangladesh, Laos, China and Thailand. It has 1,930 kilometres of coastline, and a horseshoe-shaped ring of mountains forming a natural border. The eastern part of the country is made up of a large, high, flat area known as the Shan Plateau. Below are the central lowlands, where two-thirds of the population live. The central plains are known as the dry zone, while the regions where the rivers curve along and reach the sea provide fertile plains.

It is a country with abundant natural resources and a wide variety of fauna and flora.

Climate

Myanmar has a tropical climate with three seasons: hot season (March through April), rainy season (May through October) and the cool season (November through February). The monsoon pattern brings heavy rain and certain areas are susceptible to flooding. The climate varies by region, with cooler temperatures in the mountains.

Fast Fact

Hkakabo Rizi is noHkakabo Razi is not only Myanmar's highest point, at 5,881 metres, but also the highest point in Southeast Asia

Fabulous Fauna

Myanmar is well known for its rich variety of flora and fauna. Myanmar's coasts are largely undisturbed. As a result, it is also home to some of Southeast Asia's most extensive and least disturbed coastal and marine ecosystems, which include coral reefs, mangroves and seagrass beds. All told, over 800 marine fish species are found here, as well as nine seagrass species and 51 corals.

Myanmar has about 300 mammal species, some of which are listed as vulnerable or critically endangered. About 1,031 bird species are in Myanmar, as well as many unique amphibians, reptiles and insects.

Some of Myanmar's Critically Endangered animals are:

- White-bellied heron
- Baer's Pochard
- Spoon-billed Sandpiper
- Sumatran Rhinoceros
- Hawksbill turtle
- Fish-eating crocodile
- Flatback tortoise
- Irrawaddy river shark
- Arakan forest turtle
- Slender-billed vulture
- White-rumped vulture
- Sunda pangolin
- Black ibis
- Javan rhinoceros
- Myanmar snub-nosed monkey
- Helmeted hornbill
- Pink-headed duck
- Red-headed vulture

Red-headed vulture

Myanmar snub-nosed monkey

The Myanmar snub-nosed monkey was only discovered in 2010. It is found in Myanmar and China.

Tourism and Major Sites

Tourism is an emerging contributor to Myanmar's economy. There is so much to see, from stunning beaches and bustling cities, to visiting northern hill tribes and ancient ruins. It is no wonder that Myanmar has been predicted to be Asia's next big destination.

There were well over 3 million foreign visitors in 2017. Thailand, China and Japan are the top three visitor countries. 32,628 Australians visited Myanmar; that's triple the amount who visited in 2011.

Myanmar's former capital and its largest city is a busy city, with a historic heart. It is the country's economic and artistic centre.

Its most famous landmark is Shwedagon Pagoda, a 99-metre gold plated stupa that can be seen from all over the city. According to legend, the pagoda is more than 2,500 years old dating back to the lifetime of the Buddha, making it the oldest pagoda in Myanmar, and certainly its most important Buddhist site.

The area known as Bagan was once a powerful ancient capital, and now one of Myanmar's most important tourist attractions. Between the 11th and 13th centuries, at the height of the empire's power, more than 10,000 temples were built. Today, about 2,200 monuments remain in various states of repair, which makes Bagan one of the densest concentrations of temples and pagodas in the world.

This 21 kilometre long, 11 kilometre wide lake is a place of extraordinary beauty, and ecological importance. Over 200 monasteries dot the lake, along with the ruins of ancient stupas. Villages line the lake, with locals living much like they have for generations.

Important Sites

As of 2017, there is one UNESCO World Heritage site in Myanmar, and another 14 sites on the tentative list.

The World Cultural Heritage Site on the list is:
- **Pyu Ancient Cities**

Transport

There are several modes of transport in Myanmar, but a great deal of work needs to be done to make each method of travel safer. Infrastructure has improved in recent years, with countries like Japan and South Korea offering aid or low-cost loans to give their companies access to these large scale projects. Around 72% of household cars, trucks and vans are in urban areas compared to 28% in rural areas, where 29% of households still use bullock-drawn carts.

Getting Around

Myanmar has 27,000 kilometres of road, but only 3,200 kilometres are paved. There is only one expressway, the 590 km Yangon-Mandalay highway, which has four concrete surface lanes. The government has plans to build around 34,400 km of roads over the next 20 years.

Towns offer a variety of city buses, motorcycle taxis, rickshaws and modern Japanese pick-up trucks. There are public buses in cities such as Yangon and Mandalay. In 2017, Yangon launched a new bus network system to help two million daily commuters.

Railways

The first railway was introduced in 1877, when Burma was a British colony. Myanmar Railways now oversees just over 5,000 kilometers of railroad tracks. Infrastructure is generally poor and parts of the tracks aren't passable during monsoon season. There are 858 stations throughout the country, with Yangon Central and Mandalay Central being the main stations.

Air

Myanmar has three international airports, Yangon (RGN), Mandalay (MDL) and Naypyidaw (NYT). There are domestic airports in numerous other regions including Bagan and Heho / Inle Lake. The national airline is Myanmar Airways International, but the country has more than a dozen registered airlines.

Water Transport

Myanmar has three sea ports and five river ports. The government has announced plans to build six more inland maritime port terminals – four on the Irrawaddy River and two on the Chindwin River. This would improve navigation channels and boost river transport, offering a low cost freight option and about 4,587 kilometres of navigable water routes; primarily the Mekong and its tributaries. A further 3,000 kilometres of waterways is navigable to smaller boats.

Flags, Symbols and Emblems

Flag of Myanmar

The current flag of Myanmar was adopted along with a new constitution in 2010. It is composed of a large white five-pointed star centred on three horizontal stripes in red, green and yellow. Yellow symbolises solidarity between people, green stands for natural wealth of the country, and red represents courage. The white star symbolizes hope in the unity for all people of Myanmar.

National Anthem

The national anthem of Myanmar is Kaba Ma Kyei.

National Flower

The national flower of Myanmar is the padauk.

National Animal

Both the green peafowl and the white elephant are national animals.

National Instrument

Saung-Gauk (Burmese harp) is the national musical instrument of Myanmar.

National Sport

1,500-year-old Chinlone (caneball) is the national sport of Myanmar.

Find Out More

Primary and Secondary Sources

A primary source is information created by someone who was a part of or witnessed the historical event first hand. Primary sources are very important to historians researching events and time periods. Examples of primary sources are letters, emails, filmed interviews and clips, journals and diaries, census statistics, government documents, art and maps (from the time period), the news (both print and film), photographs and modern maps.

A secondary source is when someone who did not actually witness the event retells the facts that someone else told them. Examples of secondary sources include news (both print and film), interviews, letters, journals and diaries, biographies, textbooks and paraphrased quotations.

Primary and Secondary Source Search

An estimated 706,000 Rohingya have fled Myanmar to Bangladesh since August 2017. Can you find primary and secondary sources about this event?

READ

- *I See the Sun in Myanmar* by Dedie King
- *Bamboo People* by Mitali Perkins

Search Key Words

Myanmar, Burma, Yangon, Bagan, Inle Lake, Irrawady, Ayeyarwady, Aung San Suu Kyi, Rohingya

Glossary

BUDDHISM: a religion based on the teachings of Buddha
CULTURE: practices, beliefs and customs of a society or people
DIALECT: a variation of a language unique to a region
ENDANGERED: when a species is at risk
ETHNIC GROUP: people who share a common culture, language and heritage

HIGHLANDS: a mountainous or elevated region
MONSOON: a season of heavy rain
PLATEAU: large, flat area found in higher regions
SUSTAINABILITY: to support the environment
STIPEND: a fixed regular sum paid as salariy
TROPICAL: hot, humid climate
TYPHOON: a powerful tropical storm

Index